EXTREME
WEATHER

Margaret Hynes

KINGFISHER

KINGFISHER

First published 2011 by Kingfisher
an imprint of Macmillan Children's Books
a division of Macmillan Publishers Limited
20 New Wharf Road, London N1 9RR
Basingstoke and Oxford
Associated companies throughout the world
www.panmacmillan.com

Consultant: Dr Mike Goldsmith

Illustrations by: The Peter Bull Art Studio – Peter Bull
The Art Agency – Mick Posen, Mark Garlick
Linden Artists – Steve & Sam Weston, Seb Quigley

ISBN 978-0-7534-3071-2

7 9 8 6
6TR/0312/UG/WKT/140MA

A CIP catalogue record for this book is available from the British Library.

Printed in China

Note to readers: The website addresses listed in this book are correct at the time of publishing.
However, due to the ever-changing nature of the internet, website addresses and content can change.
Websites can contain links that are unsuitable for children. The publisher cannot be held responsible for
changes in website addresses or content, or for information obtained through third-party websites.
We strongly advise that internet searches should be supervised by an adult.

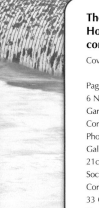

The Publisher would like to thank the following for permission to reproduce their material. Every care has been taken to trace copyright holders. However, if there have been unintentional omissions or failure to trace copyright holders, we apologise and will, if informed, endeavour to make corrections in any future edition (t = top, b = bottom, c = centre, r = right, l = left):

Cover: Shutterstock/1000 Words; Back Cover: Alamy/Tom Viggers.

Pages 4tr Getty/Stephen Jaffe; 4bc Corbis/Theo Allofs; 5tc Corbis/epa; 5cl Press Association(PA)/AP; 5cr Nature PL/Marguerite Smits van Oyen; 5bl Frank Lane Picture Agency (FLPA)/Frans Lanting; 6 NASA/JPL/ISS; 7 Shutterstock/Susie Prentice; 8cr Corbis/Jim Reed; 9tl Shutterstock/Jhaz Photography; 9tc NASA/JPL/ISS; 9 Photolibrary/Peter Arnold Images; 9bc Corbis/Jim Reed; 10–11 Corbis/Wallace Garrison/Monsoon; 10tc Corbis/Matt Sullivan/Reuters; 10tc Shutterstock/Jhaz Photography; 10tr Alamy/Thierry Grun; 11tr Science Photo Library (SPL)/Peter Menzel; 11cr Shutterstock/Image Team; 11bc Corbis/Scott Stulberg; 12–13 Alamy/A.T. Willett; 12tr Corbis/Jim Reed/Science Faction; 12c Shutterstock/Franc Podgorsek; 12bl Shutterstock/Alexander Ozerov; 13t Corbis/David Crosling; 13tr Reuters/China Photos; 13b Corbis/Wojtek Kaminski; 14 Shutterstock/Dark o; 15tc SPL/Jim Reed; 15r SPL/Howard Bluestein; 16c Alamy/Kevin Howchin; 18–19 Getty/AFP; 18c PA/AP; 19tr PA/Dav Raj Pant/AP; 19cl Getty/Sean Gallup; 19br PA Wire/Barry Batechelor/AP; 20tl PA/Robert F. Bukaty/AP; 20 Shutterstock/Antonio S.; 20br Shutterstock/Demid; 20cr Corbis/Henrik Trygg; 20tr Corbis/Larry W. Smith; 21cl Getty/Dan Rafla/Aurora; 21c Blue Green Images; 21b Shutterstock/Four Oaks; 21r Getty/Franz Aberham; 22tr Getty/Adrian Pope; 22c PA/Rajes Kumar Singh/AP; 22bl Alamy/RADIANCE; 23br PA/AP; 24 Getty/National Geographic Society; 25c Getty/Imagebank; 25tr Corbis/Kazuyoshi Nomachi; 26cl Corbis/Bob E Daemmrich; 26tr Trevor/ Met. Office Australia; 26b SPL/NASA; 26–27t NASA; 27 SPL/NASA; 27bl Shutterstock/Seti; 27br Corbis/Reuters; 28–29 NASA/JPL; 29tl Getty/Ted Soqui/Flickr; 29c Getty/AFP; 29cr PA/AP; 29bl Reuters/Tim Wimbourne; 29br Shutterstock/Melvin Lee; 30 Shutterstock/dinadesign; 32 Corbis/Steve Kaufman; 33 Getty/Mandel Ngan; 34–35 Shutterstock/kavram; 34cr Corbis/Christine Schneider; 34br Alamy/imagebroker; 35tc Shutterstock/Lars Lindblad; 35c Shutterstock/vesilvio; 35bc WaterAid/Newah; 35bl Photolibrary/John Woodworth; 36–37 NASA; 36tr SPL/Jim Reed; 36bl SPL/SFR; 36bc NOAA; 37t NOAA; 37c Corbis/ Jim Edds/ Jim Reed; 38cl Shutterstock/cardiae; 38t & 38–39 & 39tl NASA; 39c Corbis/Ashley Cooper; 39cr SPL/British Antarctic Survey; 40tl Getty/ChinaFotoPress; 40tc Corbis/Najlah Feanny; 40tr PA/AP/David J. Phillip; 40c Getty/UN.MINUSTAH; 40br PA/AP; 41 PA/AP; 41bc PA/AP/Paloa Crociana; 42tr Alamy/Photoshot; 42bl Corbis/Frederic Soltan; 42br Photoshot/Shafiqul Islam/WpN; 43tl Alamy/David Gordon; 43tr Corbis/Skyscan; 43bl Alamy/StockShot; 43br Getty/AFP; 48tr Alamy/Jeff Greenberg; 48cl Alamy/David R. Frazier Photolibrary; 48cr Getty/Time & Life Pictures/Ted Russell; 48bl Alamy/Arcticphoto; 48bl Shutterstock/Ilona Baha.

CONTENTS

WEATHER WORLD

You may not realize it, but the weather has a huge influence on your life. It affects what you wear, the type of house you live in and the food you eat. Weather is the condition of the lowest level of the atmosphere, called the troposphere, at a given time and place. The weather is determined by such things as temperature, air pressure, humidity and wind. While the weather whips up waves at sea and even carves rocks over time, extremes of the weather are more fearsome, creating many of the world's worst disasters.

1

The fierce, twisting winds of a tornado flatten everything in their path.

2

"If you spend your whole life waiting for the storm, you'll never enjoy the sunshine."

Morris West (1916–99)
Australian novelist

Drought

Around the world, different areas receive different amounts of rain. When an area receives much less rain than usual, or no rain at all, the region is experiencing a drought. During a drought, once-fertile soil may turn to dust and rivers may dry up, leaving only a cracked riverbed.

Extreme conditions

While tropical regions roast under the searing sun, polar regions freeze under a thick layer of ice. The hot, moist weather of some places builds savage storms, such as hurricanes and tornadoes. Heavy rainfall can lead to floods and unusually low rainfall causes droughts. Hazards in cold parts of the world include blizzards and avalanches.

> Meteorologists (weather scientists) issued the first-ever weather forecasts in 1869, in the USA.

Some farmers wear woven rain shields called krups, as protection against the relentless rain, and so that they can keep their hands free for working.

An avalanche's rolling mass of snow engulfs a ski chalet in the European Alps.

Penguins huddle together for warmth during Antarctic blizzards.

Salt miners work in the relatively cooler mornings and evenings, rather than the baking heat of the middle of the day.

KEY

1 Known as Tornado Alley, this part of the USA has more tornadoes than anywhere else on Earth.

2 The Atacama desert, South America, contains sites that are the driest places on our planet.

3 The European Alps can suffer avalanches during heavy snowfall.

4 Antarctica is the coldest and windiest place on Earth.

5 Danakil Depression, Ethiopia, is the hottest inhabited place in the world.

6 Cherrapunji, India, is among the wettest places on Earth.

WEATHER MACHINE

Earth's weather is controlled by the sun. It heats air masses in different parts of the globe, making them lighter and causing them to rise through the atmosphere. Cool air rushes in to fill the gap and we feel this movement of air as wind. The heat of the sun also helps water vapour to form and move to create rain, snow or thunderstorms. Earth is heated unevenly by the sun, but global winds and ocean currents redistribute the heat around the world, helping to prevent severe extremes of temperature.

Atmospheric pressure

Air pressure is greatest near the ground, because there is a larger weight of air pushing down from above. The higher in the atmosphere you go, the less air and air pressure there is.

sun's rays hit the poles at an angle

Earth is tilted at an angle of 23.5 degrees

sun's rays hit Earth at different angles

Solar power

The power of the sunlight a region receives depends on the angle at which the sun hits it. Towards the poles, the sun's rays come in at such a shallow angle that they are spread and weakened, which is why polar regions are cold. But in the tropics, the rays can strike from directly overhead, so the tropical regions are warm. In the day, the sun is weakest at dusk and dawn, when it sets and rises. It is at its strongest in the middle of the day, when it shines down most directly.

KEY

▬	▬	▬
the polar regions, where it is cold	the tropics, where it is warm	the equator, where it is hottest

side of the globe facing away from the sun is in darkness

> The sun's core temperature is 15 million°C and its surface temperature is 5,500°C.

"The Earth has received the embrace of the sun and we shall see the results of that love."

Sitting Bull (c. 1831–90)
Hunkpapa Lakota Sioux leader and holy man

sun's rays hit the equator straight on

⊖ MOVING WATER AND AIR

Water cycle

Moisture rises up from the Earth's surface and falls back down again in a never-ending cycle driven by the sun's energy. As the sun heats the surface of lakes and oceans, moisture evaporates, turning into an invisible gas called water vapour. This rises into the air, where cooler temperatures high up cause the vapour to condense as clouds, and then to fall back to Earth as rain, snow or hail.

cooling vapour forms clouds

clouds carried inland by winds

water falls as rain

water vapour rises from ocean

plants lose water to air

water returns to ocean

Earth rotates in an anti-clockwise direction

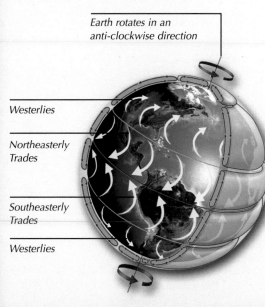

Westerlies

Northeasterly Trades

Southeasterly Trades

Westerlies

World winds

Together, the sun's heat and Earth's rotation create global patterns of wind. Moist air at the equator, warmed by the sun, rises into the atmosphere. It then spreads north and south, raining most of its moisture over the wet tropics. Further north and south, the now dry air sinks, creating dry conditions. Some of the air flows back to the equator. The rest flows towards the poles until it meets cold, polar air. The warmer air rises again and re-circulates into the atmosphere.

southern hemisphere is tilted towards the sun, which means it is summer there

THUNDEROUS STORMS

You can be sure it will rain if dark, grey clouds fill the sky. The clouds are dark because they are so full of water that sunlight cannot pass through them. If the clouds grow into a giant anvil shape with a dark, flat base, topped by columns of lighter clouds, a thunderstorm is on the way. Such clouds are called cumulonimbus, and they generate a huge amount of energy, which is released in the form of updraughts and bursts of electricity. Storm clouds produce thunder, lightning, strong winds and heavy rain or snow.

Supercell

Most thunderstorms develop from updraughts, or cells of rising air. Particularly large and energetic, rotating updraughts – in which air rises more quickly than normal – are called supercells. These carry a huge amount of water up into the thundercloud. Supercells produce tornadoes and waterspouts.

⊜ BIRTH OF A STORM CLOUD

Warm, moist air rises and cools, causing its water vapour to condense into droplets that form a cumulus cloud. Condensation releases latent heat, which makes the air rise further and the cloud grow taller. When the droplets in the cloud become heavy enough to fall, precipitation begins and the air cools, causing a downdraught that breaks up the cloud.

1. Warm updraughts rise to create cumulus clouds.

2. The cold rain, snow or hail drags air down with it, creating a cold downdraught.

3. When there is more downdraught than updraught, the cloud dissolves (breaks up).

> About 45,000 thunderstorms hit different parts of Earth each day.

The clouds stop rising and spread out as they hit a cold, dry layer of air.

Thunderclouds

A cumulonimbus cloud can reach 16km or more in the air, while its base may loom just 500m above the ground. The air inside these clouds rises and sinks in currents, travelling at 50km/h or more. Aircraft pilots steer clear of thunderclouds because the fierce currents can catapult the aircraft upwards and downwards, which could possibly cause the pilot to lose control of the aircraft.

www.eoearth.org/article/thunderstorm

giant cumulonimbus clouds

Mammatus clouds often form on the underside of cumulonimbus clouds, but scientists cannot agree on how they are formed.

ELECTRIC SKIES

When the ominous shape of a giant cumulonimbus looms, it does not take long before the sky erupts into a spectacle of zigzagging, flashing light, deafening noise and pouring rain. It looks magnificent, but lightning is also very dangerous. Around the world about 200 people a year are killed by lightning strikes. Lightning is a huge surge of electricity. It heats the air to about 30,000°C, which is five times hotter than the surface of the sun. This superheating of the air is heard as thunder.

Sporting strikes

Humans are 65 per cent water, which conducts electricity well. As a result, people standing on golf courses or other exposed sites are a good target for lightning.

Lighter, positively charged pieces of ice and water droplets are driven up towards the top of the cloud.

Great balls of fire

Sometimes, during thundery weather, a curious ball of lightning appears a few metres above the ground and then bounces around randomly. Scientists cannot agree on how this ball lightning is formed.

"Thunder is good, thunder is impressive; but it is lightning that does all the work."

Mark Twain (1835–1910)
American novelist

Heavier, negatively charged water droplets and pieces of ice build up at the base of the cloud.

Lightning generator

Air currents inside a cumulonimbus cloud cause ice crystals or water droplets within the cloud to crash into each other, creating electrical charges – like rubbing a balloon against your hair. The bottom of the cloud becomes negatively charged. The ground and cloud top are positively charged. These charges build up and when the difference is big enough, electricity darts around. At first, lightning flashes are created inside the cloud. Then, bolts of lightning dart from the cloud to the ground.

Lightning flashes within the cloud are called sheet lightning.

Lightning bolts begin when a small stroke, known as a leader stroke, zigzags to the ground.

> CONDUCTOR - *a substance that allows electricity to pass through it easily*

A massive surge of lightning, known as the return stroke, shoots up the path created by the leader stroke.

The ground is positively charged.

TURNED TO STONE

A bolt of lightning can heat the ground to about 1,800°C in less than 100,000th of a second. If a bolt of lightning strikes dry sand, it melts and fuses the sand in the electricity's path. Once it cools, the molten sand can form curious, tubular, branch-like formations called fulgurites. The outer surfaces of fulgurites are often covered with unfused sand grains, which create a texture like sandpaper. The inner surfaces are usually smooth and glassy.

a cooled and hardened fulgurite, created from sand fused by a lightning strike

Lightning conductors

Lightning tends to strike tall objects, so skyscrapers are struck regularly. Most have metal rods called lightning conductors on their roofs. The rods protect the building by conducting the electricity safely to the ground.

Never take shelter under a tree during a storm. The moist layer below a tree's bark acts as a conductor, making trees vulnerable to lightning strikes.

❯ Although thunder is the sound of lightning, we do not hear it right away because light travels much faster than sound.

∨ CLOUD-SEEDING – the use of silver iodide, dry ice or other substances to artificially alter precipitation

ICY FALLS

Dodging hard lumps of ice hurtling from the sky at up to 170km/h is not easy – hailstones pelt anything and everything in the vicinity. They form when winds toss ice crystals up, above the freezing level in a thundercloud, and down again. Each time the ice rises, a new layer of ice forms around it. The more turbulent the storm cloud, the larger the hailstone becomes before it falls to the ground. Most hailstorms unleash pea-sized hailstones, but some produce ice lumps the size of grapefruit.

This cross-section of a hailstone reveals its internal structure of alternating layers of ice. Each layer represents a round trip to the top of a storm cloud and back down again.

car roof is severely dented by falling ice

people and cars making their way through a violent hailstorm in Sydney, Australia

hailstones smash straight through windscreen

Crushed crops

Vast regions of cropland in the USA, China, Russia and other parts of Europe are under constant threat of damage from hailstorms. Here, pea-sized hailstones have flattened a crop of gourd.

Hail havoc

Umbrellas offer little protection against pounding hailstones the size of golf balls. Such hailstones are hard enough to wipe out crops, damage buildings, cars and aircraft, and seriously injure people. This is what happened in Sydney in 1999 during the most financially costly natural disaster in Australian history.

> The largest hailstone on record was 17.8cm in diameter and had a circumference of 47.6cm.

⊖ CLOUD BUSTER

Hailstones fall when they grow so big that their weight overcomes the strength of the storm's updraughts.

Some farmers have taken nature in hand by using a technique called cloud-seeding to reduce the size of the hailstones falling onto their crops. The farmers employ scientists to rocket chemicals into the air to create cores from which extra hailstones develop. The air becomes so full of hailstones that none of them can grow large enough to cause serious damage to the crops.

preparing to fire hail-suppression chemicals, in China

WATERSPOUT

Tornadoes that travel across a sea or lake form a swirling waterspout. These can be a hazard to small boats and they can cause saltwater rain to fall if they sweep on to land. It may look like a spout of water being sucked right up to the storm cloud, but only about a metre of water is lifted. The rest of the waterspout is formed of cloud.

A waterspout swirls across the sea.

"When a tornado strikes, all of us are at risk."

Spencer Bachus (born 1947)
American politician

Fish in lakes are lifted up with the water by the high-pressure winds.

> VORTEX – *the motion of air or a fluid swirling rapidly around a central point*

Violent vortex

Winds around the destructive vortex (spinning centre) of a tornado can move at up to 500km/h. They lift the roofs off houses and blow cars, people and animals about as if they were toys. The funnel winds, and the debris caught up in them, work like a circular saw, cutting up anything they make contact with.

All the dust and broken objects picked up by the tornado give it a dark and menacing colour.

Special Doppler radar dishes mounted on the back of trucks help scientists to see whether a vortex is forming within a cloud.

People in areas that experience many tornadoes have underground shelters or reinforced rooms at home, for protection.

THE TWISTER

If you see a swirling funnel of air descend from the base of a supercell storm cloud, get ready to witness the most extreme of all storms – a tornado – charging across the land. Tornadoes, also known as 'twisters', form when warm air is drawn in at the base of the cloud and rises upwards. As the air rises, it spins. If the spin is intense enough, the rotating air extends below the cloud base as a funnel. Tornadoes occur in North America, western Europe, eastern Asia and Australia.

> The Tri-State Tornado of 1925 killed 695 people, making it the deadliest tornado in American history.

stage one

stage two

The pressure falls as the storms start to grow and merge. As air flows towards the low-pressure zone, it picks up more energy from the warm sea surface and also starts to spin in an anti-clockwise direction.

The system takes on a circular shape once the thunderstorms merge.

High-level winds spiral outwards, blowing clockwise.

Birth of a cyclone

Tropical cyclones begin as small thunderstorms that form because the hot, tropical sun evaporates water over the ocean. If the seawater is warmer than about 27°C, several storms may cluster together and whirl around as one. The storm system grows stronger, fuelled by the warm surface water. Eventually, an area of calm – called the eye – develops at the centre and the system becomes a cyclone. When cyclones move away from the warm water, they lose their source of energy and the winds drop rapidly.

"Anyone who says they're not afraid at the time of a hurricane is either a fool or a liar, or a little bit of both."

Anderson Cooper (born 1967)
American journalist and author

TROPICAL CYCLONES

Storm surge

Hurricane winds pile up water on the ocean's surface. In addition, the storm's eye pulls up a mound of water in the calm centre of the storm. These bulges in the ocean are called storm surges and they cause flooding if they reach the land.

Furious, spiralling storms – which may be hundreds of kilometres across and with wind speeds of up to about 300km/h – develop in the tropical areas of the oceans. These storms have different names in different parts of the world, but cyclones, hurricanes and typhoons are all the same weather feature. If they cross onto the shore, it can spell disaster. This is because they bring towering waves, torrential rain and high winds that destroy buildings, cause massive flooding and kill many people.

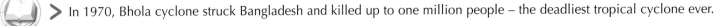

> In 1970, Bhola cyclone struck Bangladesh and killed up to one million people – the deadliest tropical cyclone ever.

stage three

Cold, dry air descends in the eye, leaving it clear of cloud.

Whether tropical cyclones spin anti-clockwise or clockwise depends whether they are in the northern or southern hemisphere.

The deadliest winds and most intense rainfall occur at the eye wall.

Warm, moist air spirals up around the wall of the hurricane's eye.

Winds at the water's surface blow anti-clockwise.

Water vapour rises up from the sea to form walls of clouds.

⊖ HURRICANE HIERARCHY

Scientists grade hurricanes from one to five according to their wind speed. The different categories cause different levels of damage when the storm reaches land. A number one storm causes mild damage, while the worst storm, a number five hurricane, causes almost total destruction.

category one
wind: 119–153km/h

category two

category three

category four

category five
wind: more than 249km/h

LEVEE – a raised, sloping embankment that is built along a river on a coast as protection against flooding

AFTERMATH

For people caught up in an extreme weather event, the passing of the weather itself does not always signal the end of their woes. Floods resulting from heavy rainfall, melting snow or storm waves swamping a coast can cause widespread devastation and account for nearly half of all deaths from natural disasters in the world. Heavy rains can also lead to deadly mudslides.

Rising river

A torrential downpour of rain caused this river in Dazhou, China, to fill beyond its capacity. The surplus water has overflowed the banks and is deluging buildings and streets, while the bridge is in danger of being swept away by the rising water.

Poor defences

As Hurricane Katrina charged across the Gulf of Mexico, USA, in August 2005, the most severe loss of life occurred in New Orleans. This was because the storm surge caused by the hurricane broke through the levee system there, leading to flooding in about 80 per cent of the city.

> About 850,000 houses were damaged or destroyed in the New Orleans flood that followed Hurricane Katrina.

Flood damage

These people are working hard to build defences against rising floodwater because they know the havoc it could cause. Floods destroy buildings, roads and bridges, as well as cutting off services such as electricity and telephones. If sewage washes into drinking water supplies, deadly waterborne diseases, such as cholera and typhoid, can spread throughout flooded communities.

About 25,000 people took refuge inside the Louisiana Superdome.

⊖ MUDSLIDES

During very heavy rainfall, rainwater mixes with soil and forms mud. If this happens on a slope, gravity can draw the mud downwards. This creates a moving river of mud known as a mudslide. Some mudslides begin quickly and continue much like an avalanche, sweeping away people and buildings in their path. Nepal, in southern Asia, is particularly prone to mudslides because the country is set on the slopes of the Himalayas, and monsoon rains drench it every year.

mudslide in Dadeldhura, Nepal, in 2009

"Great floods have flown from simple sources."

William Shakespeare (1564–1616)
English playwright,
from his play All's Well That Ends Well

Flash flood

If huge amounts of rain fall during a short period of time, a flash flood could strike. These are the most dangerous floods of all because they happen with hardly any warning, leaving people little time to protect themselves and their property. In 2004, a 3-metre-high torrent of water surged through Boscastle, England, when about 6.5cm of rain fell in just two hours.

Thousands of buildings were submerged during the flood.

Trees were uprooted and cars were upturned by the torrent of water.

AIR-SEA RESCUE

Winds disturb the surface of the oceans, whipping up waves or twisting columns of spray into waterspouts. During severe storms, winds can push waves to heights of up to 30m. Boats at sea may be capsized (overturned) or wrecked by storm waves, which batter anything in their path when they crash onto the coast. It is often in these tempestuous conditions that seafarers find themselves in need of rescue.

> HIGH SEA - *very rough sea, due to strong winds and storms*

Storm waves washed away the beach and damaged the road and houses.

Ship out of water

A storm surge can wrench boats from their moorings and smash them into each other. Sometimes, surging seawater carries boats far inland where it dumps them, leaving them high and dry when the water drains away.

High sea

With poor visibility and the distraction of crashing waves buffeting their vessel, lifeboat crews would find it difficult enough to stay afloat and keep themselves safe during a storm without also having to rescue others. In stormy conditions such as these, helicopters are deployed instead of boats. Once on the scene, the rescuer is lowered from the hovering helicopter on a winch lift to the person in trouble. The survivor is then attached to the rescuer and lifted into the helicopter, which flies directly to a hospital.

"The fishermen know that the sea is dangerous and the storm terrible, but they have never found those dangers sufficient reason for remaining ashore."

Vincent Van Gogh (1853–90)
Dutch artist

KEY

1. Helicopter hovering in safety several metres above the crashing waves

2. Winch operator winding up the winch lift

3. Injured sailor being winched to safety and medical attention

4. Waves buffeting a capsized boat

5. Capsized sailor using the daggerboard to pull her sailing dinghy upright in the water

6. Waves gouging out a cave in coastal rocks

7. Submerged rocks onto which vessels could be forced during a storm

Giant waves can overwhelm a boat and cause it to capsize.

❯ The first air-sea rescue was carried out in 1911 by Hugh Robinson, who used his seaplane to pull a crashed pilot from Lake Michigan, USA.

MONSOONS

Monsoons are strong, sometimes violent winds that change direction with the season. The land warms up more quickly than the sea, so continents are warmer than the oceans in the summer. In winter, the land goes cold more quickly than the sea, which holds on to its heat for longer. Warm air rises, drawing in wind, so monsoon winds blow from the land towards the sea in winter, and from the sea towards the land in the summer. The most prominent monsoons occur in southern Asia, Africa, Australia and the Pacific Coast.

Water of life

Indian farmers rely heavily on monsoon rains to raise their crops. These rains are the only source of water for 70 per cent of India's crops.

Ghat mountains

Spectacular clouds and torrential rains occur on the windward slopes of the Western Ghat mountains in India. Here, the early monsoon winds pile up against the steep slopes until the wind and clouds eventually roll over the peaks and take monsoon rains further inland.

Rain dance

The monsoon rains are a cause for celebration when they first arrive. By this time, people have endured six months of brutally dry, oppressive weather and the cooling rains are a welcome relief.

"The best thing one can do when it's raining is to let it rain."

Henry Wadsworth Longfellow (1807–82)
American poet

South Asian monsoon

The prevailing winds of summer blow from the Indian Ocean onto the warm Asian continent. In winter, however, the prevailing winds blow outwards from the cold land. The seasonal movement of the eastward-flowing jet stream also affects the monsoon winds. This high-level air stream blocks in warm, rising air, but the jet stream moves north in summer, allowing moist ocean winds to be drawn further into the continent.

KEY

1. Warm air rises off the baking land, drawing in a soft breeze off the cool sea

2. The eastward-flowing jet stream blocks in the rising air

3. The jet stream moves north, allowing the warm air to rise unobstructed

4. Water-laden winds stream in off the ocean

5. Ocean winds forced over the mountains cool, bringing heavy rains on the coast

6. Water-laden winds sweep northwards, bringing rain to the rest of the country

3 position of jet stream after it has moved north

HIMALAYA MOUNTAINS

2

position of jet stream in May

BANGLADESH

1

INDIA

6

4

The thickest clouds form over the Western Ghats.

5

summer monsoon in South Asia

INDIAN OCEAN

www.wrh.noaa.gov/fgz/science/monsoon.php?wfo=fgz

◉ AFTER THE DELUGE

While farmers and those hoping for the end of the dry summer await the monsoon rains anxiously, the rains can also bring great hardship. They can be so intense that they cause floods, particularly in India and Bangladesh, where the delta of the Ganges river is at risk of frequent flooding, especially if a storm surge occurs at the same time.

Flooding in Bangladesh leaves communities in chaos.

DRY LANDS

The driest places on the planet are deserts. They are dry either because it simply does not rain very much, or because the baking sun makes the air so warm that evaporation is greater than rainfall. It might surprise you to learn that polar regions are said to be deserts. This is because the air there is too cold to hold enough moisture for precipitation. Without water, deserts become harsh, hostile environments, empty of all but a few plants and animals that are adapted to life in these conditions.

Night chills

Clear skies allow the sun to scorch hot deserts by day. But with no clouds to trap in the heat, the temperature may drop to below freezing at night, so desert-dwelling people must wrap up and build fires to keep warm.

Sahara scorcher

The Sahara is the world's largest hot desert. Its centre is extremely arid (dry), with little vegetation. The highlands, and northern and southern regions of the desert, have areas of sparse grassland and desert shrubs. At midday, the temperature in the shade soars to more than 55°C. Few animals are active at this time. But, as the sun sets, many creatures emerge from under the rocks and out of their burrows.

> A region is called a desert if it usually receives 25cm or less of rain each year.

KEY

1. Rock pillars are carved into their unusual shapes by sand carried on the wind
2. Sand cat uses any available cover to protect itself from the sun
3. Cactus stores water in its swollen stem
4. Desert eagle soars above the desert, watching for prey on the ground
5. Fennec fox's burrowing and nocturnal lifestyle keeps it out of the baking sun
6. Cape hare survives in higher temperatures than most other hares
7. Strong winds blow sand and dust that sweep over the desert in a sandstorm
8. Sidewinder snake uses a wave-like motion to move efficiently across the shifting sand

Trick of the light

These camels may look like they are drinking, but what you see as water is an optical illusion, called a mirage. The shimmering, water-like reflection is created in extreme heat when light is bent as it passes the boundary between very hot air near the ground and the slightly cooler air above it.

During the day, the Sahara scorpion hides under rocks to keep out of the sun.

⊖ DESERT DISTRIBUTION

Two great belts of desert regions, including those of southwestern USA, North Africa and Australia, encircle the world in the sub-tropics either side of the equator. Deserts formed in regions sheltered from the rain by high mountains include South America's Atacama desert and Patagonia region, and Asia's Taklamakan desert. Parts of the Gobi desert lie so deep in the Asian interior that winds bearing water from the oceans dry out before they reach the parched land.

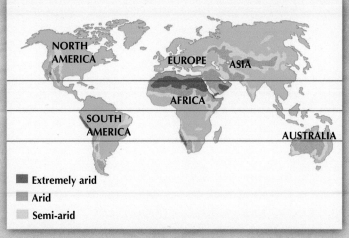

NORTH AMERICA
EUROPE ASIA
AFRICA
SOUTH AMERICA
AUSTRALIA

■ Extremely arid
■ Arid
□ Semi-arid

The world's deserts cover approximately one-third of the land.

WATER SHORTAGE

Many of us enjoy dry, sunny, cloudless days. However, unusually low rainfall for prolonged periods can lead to drought. We expect to find dry, rainless conditions in very hot places between the tropics and the equator. But these conditions also occur in regions that are too far inland for winds bearing moisture evaporated from the oceans to reach, or where mountains block winds from blowing moisture to the land beyond the peaks.

dust storm in
Melbourne, Australia

Black blizzard

When the wind blows hard over arid landscapes, it creates swirling clouds of choking, blinding sand and dust that can be carried on the wind for many kilometres. Dust storms raised in rural areas have been known to overwhelm whole cities.

Out of puff

Crops cover swathes of the Midwest region in the USA. If winds bearing moisture from the Gulf of Mexico in the south do not blow in the right direction, or with enough force, the crops can succumb to drought.

● SHIFTING STREAMS

Rivers of fast-moving winds, called jet streams, circle Earth in a meandering pattern high in the atmosphere. Jet streams separate cold polar air from warmer air and shift position with the seasons, moving tropical moisture to temperate regions. If there is a period when the jet stream weakens or follows a different path than usual, the moisture may be diverted away from where it is normally found. This results in a drought.

jet stream clouds over Egypt and the Red Sea

satellite view
of the Himalayas
and central Asia

"There struck the worst of dust storms that ever filled the sky... It fell across our city like a curtain of black rolled down."

Woody Guthrie (1912–67)
American singer-songwriter, from his 1940 song
The Great Dust Storm

> During a dust storm in Australia, in 2009, the country lost an estimated 75,000 tonnes of dust per hour to the Pacific Ocean.

http://library.thinkquest.org/03oct/01027/sandstorm.html

Parched land

The Taklamakan is a moderately warm, mid-latitude desert. The region is far inland and ringed by mountains, so precipitation is extremely low at about 24mm per year. Traditionally, camels were used to carry trade goods across this parched, sandy landscape because of their ability to last long periods without water.

Lush vegetation covers the rainy, windward side.

Arid conditions prevail on the leeward side.

Rain shadow

When winds meet mountains, the air rises to pass over the peaks. It becomes colder, causing rain to fall on that side of the mountain, known as the 'windward' side. By the time the air makes it over the mountain to the 'leeward' side, it has lost much of its vapour. This is known as the rain shadow effect. It is one of the reasons why many deserts are found on the side of a mountain range facing away from the ocean.

HIMALAYAS

A face scarf protects this woman's eyes from dust as she carries water in the Gobi desert, which sits in the rain shadow of the Himalayas.

El Niño and La Niña

The unusually warm sea created by an El Niño makes the air more humid, causing heavy rain and violent storms. Countries in the western Pacific, deprived of the warm ocean current, have very dry weather. La Niña tends to cause the opposite effects to El Niño. Where El Niño would cause a dry period, La Niña usually causes a rainy period.

"El Niño is similar to dropping a big rock in a pond, the pond in this case is the Pacific Ocean."

Jagadish Shukla (born 1944)
President of the Institute of Global
Environment and Society, USA

PACIFIC PATTERNS

El Niño and La Niña are two extremes of a Pacific Ocean-atmosphere cycle known as the El Niño-Southern Oscillation (ENSO). During an El Niño, the winds that blow west over the tropical Pacific weaken, allowing warm water to flow east. The westward-blowing winds become stronger during a La Niña, causing an abnormal amount of cold water to build up in the central and eastern Pacific. El Niño and La Niña affect world weather patterns dramatically, creating extreme conditions.

Down Under downpour

This fairground sits in a La Niña-related flood. La Niña events often bring above-average rainfall and floods to much of Australia. The tropical cyclone risk for northern Australia also increases at these times.

> El Niño, which is Spanish for 'the boy', refers to baby Jesus because the unusual weather often begins around Christmas.

WILDFIRE *a rapidly spreading fire, often in forests or wilderness that is out of control*

Turned to tinder

In times of drought, plants dry out and become more flammable, raising the risk of wildfires. During the 1999 La Niña-related drought in the USA, 92,651 wildfires burned 2.3 million hectares of land.

El Niño, October 1997

Coastal chaos

High winds and heavy rains along with abnormally high tides caused havoc in coastal California, USA, during the El Niño of the winter of 1997–98.

KEY

1 Central and western USA are plagued by wildfires during a La Niña

2 Warmer than usual water (shown in red and white) builds up in the western Pacific

3 Cooler than usual water (shown in purple) builds up in the central and eastern Pacific

4 Australia experiences heavy rainfall and flooding during a La Niña

5 Western coast of the USA suffers El Niño-related storms that can cause surges and floods

6 Cooler than usual water (shown in purple) builds up in the western Pacific

7 Papua New Guinea endures droughts, which sometimes cause wildfires, during an El Niño

8 Warmer than usual water (shown in red and white) builds up in the western Pacific

9 Peru suffers severe storms during an El Niño

Freak floods

In the winter of 1997–98, El Niño-related storms pummelled the coast of Peru, bringing heavy downpours even to places that had hardly seen rain in years. About 22,000 people fled their flooded homes, and mudslides buried entire villages.

Coral bleaching

Bleached, dead coral can indicate the presence of an El Niño. The tiny, colourful algae that live in coral survive only in certain temperatures. If the sea's temperature is higher than normal, the algae moves away and the coral dies, leaving behind its pale 'skeleton'.

POLAR EXTREMES

The frozen polar regions at opposite ends of Earth receive less sunlight than anywhere else in the world. They are the coldest places on the planet. The southern region, Antarctica, is ravaged by hurricane-force winds, making it so inhospitable that the only humans who live there are scientists working in research stations. The Arctic in the north is slightly warmer, though bitterly cold compared with other places.

A weather balloon carries instruments up into the atmosphere to measure air pressure and temperature.

A face mask and goggles protect the researcher from the glare of the snow and blizzards.

Antarctic landscape and research station

Extreme-cold clothing consists of windproof outer layers, and under layers made of breathable materials.

Flagpoles are almost bent to the ground by the wind, which can reach up to 200km/h.

Strong winds create a wind chill, making the area feel colder than it really is.

> A total of 30 countries operate seasonal and permanent research stations in Antarctica.

Antarctic research

Scientists monitor Antarctica's weather and the sea ice because they affect the world's weather. Winds that constantly circle Antarctica drive storms across the ocean around it, and beyond. In winter, the surface of the ocean freezes, leaving behind salt. Some of the remaining water, heavy with salt, sinks and drives deep water currents in a system that carries ocean water around the world, redistributing heat.

Specially designed ships carry out research missions at sea and resupply the scientists on land with food and equipment.

⊜ BEAR NECESSITIES

In the Arctic, large areas of once permanently frozen ocean have now become open water, with just a few scattered ice floes. Many scientists believe the ice is melting due to unusual increases in air temperature, brought about by pollution in the atmosphere. Polar bears hunt from the ice, so they are now forced to swim exhausting distances to find stable ice from which they can secure food.

polar bears hunt for food from ice floes in the Arctic Ocean

Most of the snow that falls does not melt, but acts like a mirror, reflecting many of the incoming solar rays back into space.

Dense plumage and a layer of fat under their skin keep penguins warm in the bitter cold.

Large cracks, called fissures, appear as a slab of snow begins to break away from its surroundings.

A snowflake's symmetrical shape can be seen through a microscope. No one has ever found two snowflakes that look the same.

Snowed in

Snow is mostly air, so it is light enough to be carried on the wind in drifts. The wind piles up drifts of snow against any obstacles, such as cabins, trains and cars. These may become completely covered, trapping people inside them.

SNOW HAZARDS

A snowy landscape may look magical, but snow can be deadly. Heavy snowfall can bury buildings or make roads impassable. Snow and strong winds cause blizzards, which reduce visibility, increasing the risk of crashes and people getting lost. Mountain snow can shift and crash down, wiping out skiers, trees and even buildings.

> **VISIBILITY** - *the distance at which an object can be seen clearly*

> "No snowflake in an avalanche ever feels responsible."

Voltaire (1694–1778)
French philosopher and writer

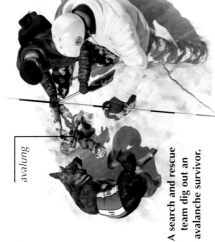

avalung

A search and rescue team dig out an avalanche survivor.

To the rescue

Teams use dogs and snow probe poles to locate buried avalanche victims, but the rescuers also rely on the survivors to use beacons to summon the team to the right area. A person can last one hour completely buried if they breathe oxygen through an 'avalung' breathing apparatus (above).

Rescue dogs help with the search for avalanche survivors.

Rescuers carry transceivers that pick up signals from distress beacons.

White-out

If snowstorms last for several hours, and combine high winds with low visibility, the result is known as a blizzard. These can involve large amounts of falling snow or fallen snow that is stirred up by high winds.

Avalanche!

Snow can suddenly break loose on a steep mountainside and crash downslope in an avalanche, which collects more snow as it tumbles. Avalanches can reach speeds of 130km/h, sometimes enveloping entire villages. They are triggered by fresh snowfall, strong winds, vibrations or changes in temperature.

> During the winter of 1951–52, 649 avalanches in the European Alps killed about 265 people in what was known as the Winter of Terror.

POLLUTANTS – *things in the environment that damage the health of people or other living things*

Cloaked in clouds

During August, the Golden Gate Bridge, which spans the San Francisco Bay in the USA, is draped in fog for most of the day. The fog forms when cold air – created by a coldwater current travelling south through the Pacific from the Arctic – rolls in from the ocean and mixes with warm, summer air in the bay area. The cold air causes vapour in the warm air to condense into fog.

Clouds of smoke

Smoke plus fog makes 'smog', such as in the days when fog mixed with smoke from coal-burning homes and factories. Today, smog is a mixture of air pollutants that hang in the air, usually around big cities. Smog can cause health problems, such as irritation to the eyes, nose and throat. Long-term exposure to smog can lead to serious lung problems.

businessman wearing a mask to protect himself from smog in Tokyo, Japan

GROUND CLOUDS

Unless they have radar, ships must move cautiously or not at all in fog.

It is possible that you have literally had your head in the clouds without realizing it, as fog is a type of cloud. It forms near the ground when the air there is full of moisture and the temperature drops. If you cannot see beyond 1,000m through the suspended particles of moisture, the obstruction is considered to be a fog. Otherwise, it is called mist. Sometimes, what appears to be thick fog in the air is, in fact, a much more sinister haze called smog.

> The Grand Banks off the island of Newfoundland, Canada, is the foggiest place in the world with more than 200 foggy days a year.

"Fair is foul, and foul is fair:
hover through the fog and filthy air."

William Shakespeare (1564–1616)
English playwright, from his play Macbeth

www.crh.noaa.gov/jkl/?n=fog_types

Delayed departures

Aircraft are at their most vulnerable during take-off and landing, when the scope for making unplanned manoeuvres is limited. So, when visibility is severely reduced due to fog at an airport, planes are grounded. Any aircraft trying to land there are diverted to a fog-free airport.

Hill fog

Low cloud that sits below the top of hills or mountains is known as hill fog or upslope fog. It is formed as mild, moist air meets a hill or mountain obstacle and is forced to climb up it. As the air moves up it cools down, causing the moisture in the air to condense and form a cloud.

Treacherous travel

In very thick fog, you may not be able to see beyond a few metres. Travelling in conditions such as these is highly dangerous and accidents are common. Most ships and aircraft use radar to locate their position in relation to other craft. The fog-penetrating light in lighthouses warns ships away from rocks.

⊖ FOG COLLECTORS

Although the northern coast of Chile is enveloped in a shroud of thick cloud, known locally as 'camanchaca', the cloud does not have enough moisture to produce rain and the region is extremely dry. Some villages have put up fog nets to collect the fog water. The nets are supported by a post at either end and positioned at a right-angle to the wind. Water droplets collect on the net and fall under the force of gravity into a gutter. This directs the water into a storage tank, from where the villagers can collect the water.

**Water collection nets in Chungungo
provide the villagers with a water supply.**

**Shrouded in fog, the
light from a lighthouse
guides ships to safety.**

WEATHER WATCH

Hurricanes and other extreme weather events cannot be prevented, but with warning people may have time to protect themselves, their animals and their property. The meteorological measurements used to predict extreme weather come from a wide range of sources, such as land-based weather stations, sea-based research ships, floating weather buoys, airborne balloons and specially designed aircraft. Satellites out in space beam back pictures, monitor temperature and cloud patterns, and even measure wave heights.

⊖ RADAR RAIN MAP

A special type of Doppler radar is used to probe storm clouds. Raindrops, snow crystals and hailstones within the clouds reflect some of the radio waves back to the radar, which converts them into maps such as this one. The precipitation type is indicated by colours, which are shown here in the scale on the right. Looking down the scale, the colours indicate increasingly heavy precipitation: green is light rain, white is heavy rain and the bottom colours are hail.

a colour map of rain data generated by a Doppler radar

Thousands of land-based stations feed information to 13 central weather centres.

Engineers fit weather buoys with equipment that transmits readings back to the land, via satellites.

> The first-ever weather satellite, *Vanguard 2*, was launched in 1959.

www.fema.gov/kids/huhunt.htm

Hurricane hunter

When dangerous-looking storm clouds appear, hurricane-hunting pilots take to the skies, flying over and even through storms and hurricanes. Equipment on board the aircraft takes pictures and measurements inside the storm. Often, the crew drop mini weather stations on parachutes into the eye wall to measure conditions such as temperature, humidity and wind speed at different heights.

U.S. AIR FORCE

Some research aircraft fly right through the eye of the storm.

Scientists on board the aircraft use specialist equipment to navigate their way through storms, recording data as they go.

Hurricane surveillance

A developing hurricane is under constant observation by satellites in space, special aircraft and Doppler radar on the ground. Satellite images show the track of a hurricane. Meanwhile, the radar provides information for estimating rainfall and monitors the bands of rain, the hurricane's eye and the eye wall around it (see illustration on page 17). The aircraft gather data on air pressure and storm size. In addition, buoys floating on the oceans relay information about water temperatures that could fuel the hurricane.

"Prediction is very hard, especially when it is about the future."

Lawrence Peter "Yogi" Berra (born 1925)
American baseball legend

Melting away

In just five weeks, during the Antarctic summer of 2002, a 3,200km² section of the Larsen B ice shelf broke up and floated off into the Weddell Sea as icebergs. The 220m-thick mass of floating ice had been stable for 12,000 years before its collapse. This was caused by increasing temperatures in the region, which has seen a 2.5°C temperature rise over the past 50 years.

Larsen B shelf on 31 January 2002

The ice shelf is a floating extension of an ice sheet on the land.

Coal

Over the last 100 years or so, we have enjoyed a technological revolution powered by fossil fuels, particularly coal. When they are burned, fossil fuels release carbon dioxide into the atmosphere.

CLIMATE CHANGE

Clues to the climates of the distant past can be found in rocks, fossils and the polar ice sheets. These show that throughout Earth's history there were times that, when averaged, world surface temperatures were either lower or higher than today's average. The past 100 years have seen an unusually rapid increase in the average global temperature. This is known as global warming and it seems to coincide with an increase in carbon dioxide emissions created by human activity. Many scientists predict global warming could have catastrophic effects.

> About 90 per cent of the world's ice is on Antarctica. Global sea levels would rise by 61m if this ice melted.

Bird's-eye view

NASA launched the NOAA-6 weather satellite in 1979. It has been instrumental in the mapping of ice in the polar regions since it was delivered into orbit. The maps provide a vivid record of the deterioration of the polar ice caps as a result of climate change.

Rising sea levels

Some scientists predict global warming could make Earth's climate about 2.5°C warmer during the 21st century. This heat could cause seawater to warm up and expand, raising sea levels. If this happens, many islands that lie only 1m to 2m above sea level could simply disappear.

Funafuti Island in the Pacific Ocean

The scientists use a hollow drill bit to extract the ice core.

http://www.epa.gov/climatechange/kids/

Preserved in ice

The thick ice sheets in the polar regions built up over thousands of years. Pockets of air and particles of pollen and dust, trapped in the ice back when it first formed, provide valuable information about past climates. This helps scientists to make predictions about future climates. Researchers use drills to extract columns, or cores, of ice from the ice sheets for analysis.

Larsen B shelf on 7 March 2002

⊖ UPS AND DOWNS

During most of Earth's history, the planet was warmer than it is now, but with icy periods in between, called ice ages. Most of these climate changes developed naturally and over extremely long periods of time. However, the last century has seen an average global air temperature rise of nearly 0.8°C, which is dramatic if you consider that the world has warmed by only 4°C in the last 2,000 years.

KEY: mya = million years ago

warmer

present temp

colder

| 4,600mya | 570mya | 225mya | 65mya | 2mya |

CLEAN-UP

First, workers rescue survivors trapped under ruins by carefully clearing rubble by hand and with diggers. If there is flooding, the emergency services use powerful pumps to drain off the excess water. Later, the debris is cleared and buildings are made safe. Bridges and roads are rebuilt to allow easy movement in and out of the sites so that reconstruction can begin fully.

rescuing trapped survivors

draining floodwater with a pump

reconstructing bridges and roads

DISASTER RELIEF

Weather-related disasters such as tornadoes, hurricanes or mudslides are usually over in a few minutes in a given location. But it can take months, even years, to repair the damage they cause. When extreme weather strikes, relief workers race to the affected area and immediately set about searching for survivors among the ruined buildings. Injured people are rushed to hospital, while other survivors are given shelter, water and food. Over time, the debris is cleared and buildings are reconstructed.

Water tanks

Even during a flood, when water is everywhere, clean drinking water is often in short supply. Relief workers must install temporary water tanks to provide fresh and safe drinking water for those who need it.

Tents and living equipment were provided for these victims of the 1984 Ethiopian drought.

Temporary homes

One of the first concerns of relief workers is to provide shelter for those left without homes by the disaster. The homeless may be temporarily housed together in a large building, or each family may be provided with a tent and essential survival equipment, such as blankets, matches and food.

> STAPLE FOOD - the main food eaten and the main source of energy in somebody's diet

Emergency supplies

If disaster strikes a remote or inaccessible location, the quickest way to get aid there is usually to drop it from the sky. Where possible, the relief workers seal off a drop zone to ensure the falling parcels do not injure people on the ground. The parcels contain staple foods, such as wheat, flour, rice, pulses and powdered milk. Sometimes, the parcels also contain medical supplies and blankets.

Armed forces personnel and equipment are usually called in to help with the relief effort.

Helicopters can make more precise drops than aircraft.

Flood victims rush for food parcels in Andhra Pradesh state, India, in 2009.

Protective packing cushions the parcel's contents from the force of the impact with the ground.

> In 2007, the EU and its member states gave £768 million ($1.1 billion) in emergency relief, making the EU the world's largest aid donor.

DAMAGE LIMITATION

Hurricanes, tornadoes and other extreme weather events cannot be prevented, but the damage they cause can be limited. Weather centres broadcast warnings so that people can take refuge in specially designed shelters, or even leave the region if they can. Flood and avalanche management strategies often involve the creation of barriers, which are designed to hold back the deluge, preventing it from reaching settlements and people. Some of these defences are inspired by those found in nature.

Dune planting

Sand dunes protect coasts from storm surges, while vegetation on the dunes keeps them stable. Dune plants damaged by beach users and grazing animals are replaced as part of coastal protection projects, such as the one shown here.

Hurricane shelter

About three-quarters of the southern Asian country of Bangladesh is only 10m above sea level. Flooding is frequent, especially during the monsoon season between June and September, and the typhoon (hurricane) season of August to November. Some communities have built large shelters, which are raised above the ground on stilts so that flood waters can pass beneath them. The shelters are also designed to withstand hurricane-force winds.

hurricane shelter in Bangladesh

> The Thames Barrier closed four times in the 1980s, 35 times in the 1990s and 75 times in the first decade of this century.

The hollow gates are made of steel up to 40mm thick.

Thames Barrier, London, holding back a tidal surge

Flood barrier

Many low-lying coastal areas have concrete sea walls and flood barriers to protect them against storm and tidal surges. In the UK, the Thames Barrier protects London from surges by the North Sea. The flood gates are circular segments, which operate by rotating up and out of the water to form a barrier.

Natural buffer

Forests of salt-tolerant trees, called mangroves, grow naturally along sheltered tidal shores in tropical regions. The trees can form effective buffers that protect the land from floods. This is why this man is planting mangrove saplings on the shore.

A tangle of prop roots anchors the mangrove trees to the ground.

Snow stoppers

Mature, sturdy trees growing on a mountainside can absorb much of the energy in an avalanche, slowing it in its tracks and preventing it from doing too much damage. When there are few trees on a mountain, artificial barriers made of concrete, metal or wood can provide a similar form of protection.

www.environment-agency.gov.uk/homeandleisure/Floods/31736.aspx

GLOSSARY

avalanche
A mass of loose snow moving rapidly down a mountainside.

climate
The normal pattern of weather in a region over a long period of time.

climate change
When Earth's climate is remarkably altered as a result of natural causes or human activities.

cloud
A visible mass of condensed water vapour and/or ice particles suspended in the sky.

condense
To turn from a gas into a liquid.

cumulonimbus
A tall, dark cloud that produces heavy rain, hail and thunderstorms.

current
A ribbon of flowing ocean water.

desert
A landscape that receives very little precipitation.

downdraught
A sinking current of air.

drought
Below average rainfall over an extended period of time.

equator
An imaginary line around the middle of Earth. It separates the northern and southern hemispheres.

evaporate
To turn from a liquid into a gas.

eye
The calm, usually cloud-free centre of a hurricane.

flash flood
A flood that rises very quickly after a rainstorm.

fog
Water that has condensed from vapour into tiny droplets suspended in the air, near to the ground.

global warming
A long-term increase in the global average temperature.

hail
Rounded drops of ice that fall to the ground from storm clouds.

hemisphere
One half of the Earth. There is a northern and a southern hemisphere.

hurricane
A powerful storm that forms over the tropical parts of the ocean. In different parts of the world it is called a tropical cyclone or typhoon.

ice
Water that gets so cold that it freezes.

ice age
One of several periods in Earth's history when ice sheets covered a large part of the planet's surface.

ice sheet
A thick layer of ice that covers a very large area.

lightning
A flash of electricity in the sky.

monsoon
A seasonal change of wind that

affects the weather, especially in tropical regions where it causes wet and dry seasons.

pack ice
A large expanse of floating ice, usually at the poles.

pollution
Anything that makes air, water or earth unpleasant or unhealthy for living things.

precipitation
Moisture released from the air in the form of rain, snow, hail, fog or dew.

prevailing winds
The main direction from which winds usually blow in a certain place.

rain
Drops of water that fall from a cloud.

rainband
A long line of continuous cloud that releases heavy rain.

rain shadow
An area of decreased rainfall on the leeward side, or sheltered side, of a mountain or hill.

snow
Precipitation falling from clouds in the form of clusters of ice crystals. The crystals freeze directly from vapour without turning to raindrops.

subtropics
The regions of the Earth that lie just to the north of the Tropic of Capricorn and just to the south of the Tropic of Cancer.

supercell
A very large thundercloud with a constant rotating updraught in the middle. Supercells often produce large hail, powerful downpours, very strong winds and sometimes tornadoes.

thunder
The sound made by air as it expands during a flash of lightning.

tornado
A violent, rotating column of air that is in contact with both the ground and a cumulonimbus cloud.

trade winds
Steady, easterly winds that blow from the tropics towards the equator.

tropical cyclone
The name for a hurricane in the South Pacific and Indian Ocean.

tropics
The hot regions to the north and south of the equator, between the Tropic of Cancer and the Tropic of Capricorn.

typhoon
The name given to a hurricane in Japan.

updraught
A rising current of air.

water vapour
The invisible gas that forms when water evaporates.

waterspout
A column of spiralling air that travels across water.

weather
The conditions of the atmosphere at a certain time and place.

wind
The movement of air from one place to another.

INDEX

INVESTIGATE

We know extreme weather can be deadly, so it is always best to avoid first-hand experience of it. Find out how meteorologists predict extreme types of weather, and what people do to protect themselves from them by checking out weather centres, museums, websites and books.

Extreme weather defences

There are weather defences all around you, such as sea and river walls, flood barriers, sand dunes and coastal plants.

Wonders of the World by Philip Steele (Kingfisher)

Thames Barrier information and learning centre, 1 Unity Way, Woolwich, London, SE18 5NJ, UK

www.environment-agency.gov.uk/homeandleisure/floods/38353.aspx

Try taking part in an organized dune-planting project such as this one (above).

a meteorologist showing a visitor how he converts weather data into charts

Watch the experts

Arrange to visit a weather centre, where you can see experts at work. You can also ask them questions and find out how you can get involved in weather research.

Kingfisher Voyages: Wild Weather by Caroline Harris (Kingfisher)

Met Office, FitzRoy Road, Exeter, Devon EX1 3PB, UK

www.metoffice.gov.uk

With a simple anemometer, such as this, you would be able to take regular wind speed measurements.

Be a meteorologist

Why not monitor the weather yourself by setting up your own weather station? Books and websites are full of useful tips on how you can do this.

Weather Forecasting Made Simple by Stan Yorke (Countryside Books)

Science Museum, Exhibition Road, South Kensington, London, SW7 2DD, UK

www.bwca.cc/weather/weatherblueprints.htm

webcams broadcast live images from the research stations

Antarctic research

You don't have to endure sub-zero temperatures and blizzards to find out about Antarctic research. Simply follow the day-to-day activities of the scientists online.

Antarctica: Secrets of the Southern Continent by David McGonigal (Frances Lincoln)

Ice Station Antarctica, Natural History Museum, Cromwell Road, London, SW7 5BD, UK

www.antarctica.ac.uk/images/webcams/index.php